The Superior Cricket Watcher's
ASHES
QUIZ BOOK

The Superior Cricket Watcher's

ASHES
QUIZ BOOK

Bernard Whimpress

ISBN: 1 86476 342 6

AXIOM
AUSTRALIA

www.axiompublishers.com.au

Printed in Malaysia

Contents

PREFACE

As a boy growing up in the 1960s I was a devoted watcher of the television quiz show *Pick-A-Box*. I never thought of it then as a superior quiz show. It was a good straight quiz show with intelligent questions fired rapidly to intelligent guests, and one outstanding contestant in school-teacher Barry Jones, who went on to experience a further outstanding career in Australian public life.

For a kid like me who liked throwing spears at his teachers – i.e. lunging out of my seat with my hand up, saying 'Sir!, Sir! Please Sir!' – whenever they asked a question, the increased gimmickry and loss of a challenge on TV quiz shows has been a disappointment. Over the years, of course, I played a few games of Trivial Pursuit but the main quizzes I have engaged in have been at the cricket during idle moments or in the company of cricket history buffs in more idle moments.

Thus when Axiom Books director John Gallehawk asked me whether I would be interested in producing a cricket quiz book I was both keen and wary. Wary of asking questions which too many people would know the answers to; and keen to use the quizzes as an amusing educative tool.

The idea behind the framing of the questions is for the Intelligent Cricket Watcher to score something like 5 out of 10 or 20 out of 40 on particular topics; in other words, to know what they don't know. I don't want readers to score 10 out of 10 because that would be no test. Like a true Ashes match there ought to be a contest. Perhaps a Superior Cricket Watcher might be expected to score 7 or 8 out of 10 but any more than that and he or she should be doing their own quiz book.

I would like to think the topics chosen from Ashes to Zzzzzzz with Captains, Twelfth Men, Bradman, Bodyline, Scandals, Famous Games, Who am I's, 99s and so on in between, will offer something of a cricketing smorgasbord.

However, I also hope that not all parts of the smorgasbord will be devoured, at least not at one sitting. Ideally, the quiz will be sampled a bit at a time, with friends over ports or pints, maybe when the coming Ashes series gets under way.

Before you start may I provide one warning. The questions refer to Anglo–Australian Test cricket only so don't confuse Allan Border's 11 174 runs and Shane Warne's 583 wickets in all Tests with those against England.

Originally I wanted to set 1000 questions but 1000 good questions is a lot of work so I settled for 550. However, there are 873 answers from around 1000 possible answers and discovering these, I trust, will provide hours of pleasure.

Bernard Whimpress
Adelaide, April 2005

The
Questions

In Affectionate Remembrance
of
ENGLISH CRICKET
which died at The Oval
on
29th August 1882.
Deeply Lamented by a large circle of
Sorrowing Friends and Acquaintances
R I P
The body will be cremated
and the Ashes taken to Australia.

ASHES

1. According to myth, which Aboriginal cricketer from the 1868 side which toured England is alleged to have been cremated and his ashes placed in the Ashes urn?

2. At which venue did the 1882 Test match that came to be recognised as the original Ashes match take place?

3. Who were the Australian and English captains in the 1882 match?

4. Which Australian bowler became the first Ashes hero by taking 14 wickets for 90 runs in this game thus giving his side victory by 7 runs.

5. In which English publication did a satirical obituary notice appear on 2 September 1882 lamenting the death of English cricket and that 'the body will be cremated and the ashes taken to Australia'?
   (a) *The Times* (b) *Daily Telegraph* (c) *Sporting Times* (d) *Punch*

6. The presentation of the Ashes urn to the visiting English captain took place during the 1882-83 season. Who was the captain?
   (a) Hon. Ivo Bligh (b) Lord Harris (c) Lord Hawke

7. I was a Victorian governess who was one of a number of women who made the original presentation of the Ashes urn to the Hon. Ivo Bligh. I later married Bligh in Sunbury, Victoria in 1884. The urn was kept in the family home of Lord Darnley (as Bligh became) until his death in 1927, when it was given to Lord's. Who am I?
   (a) Florence Morphy (b) Betty Archdale (c) Rachael Heyhoe-Flint

8. Who was the Australian journalist generally credited with promoting the Ashes concept in the 1890s to cover Anglo-Australian Test matches?

9. Which English Test captain further promoted the Ashes following his 1903-04 tour of Australia after which he published a book, *How We Recovered the Ashes.*

10. What was the only occasion on which the actual Ashes urn ever left England?

The day before the first Test match,
Melbourne Cricket Ground 1877.

FIRST TEST

1. Who am I? I took the 2027 wickets at an average of 12.13 in first-class cricket in the nineteenth century and I bowled the first ball in Test cricket.

2. Charles Bannerman made the huge score of 165 retired hurt in this match. Bannerman played 44 first-class matches in a career which extended from 1870 to 1888. How many other centuries did he make? (a) 0 (b) 2 (c) 4

3. The only other batsman to pass 50 in the game was an English opener. Who was he?

4. Who am I? I was involved in prolonged dissent over an lbw decision that went against me yet my nickname was 'Happy Jack'.

5. What was an unusual feature of the Australian (6 Victorians, 5 New South Welshmen) practice sessions for this match?

6. The first Test match took place in Melbourne in March 1877. Where was the second Test played?
(a) Melbourne (b) Lord's (c) Sydney

7. Tom Horan, who batted at number three for Australia, and later captained his country, became a well known cricket writer under which nom de plume?
(a) Point (b) Third Man (c) Felix

8. James Southerton was England's oldest Test debutant and remains so. What age was he? (a) 38 years 44 days (b) 43 years 123 days (c) 49 years 119 days

9. Who made the first duck for Australia?

10. Who made the first duck for England?

CAPTAINS

1. Who was the first professional captain of England?

2. Who was English vice-captain on four tours of Australia who never captained his country there?

3. Dave Gregory was the first Australian Test captain? Where was he born?
   (a) London (b) Fairy Meadow (c) Gundagai (d) Bristol

4. Who am I? I made a century against Australia as a Cambridge University undergraduate in 1961 but did not appear in an Ashes series until 1977.

5. Who was the first amateur captain of England?

6. Who was the last amateur captain of England?

7. Name the professional captains of England before Len Hutton?

8. Which two Australian captains were born overseas?

9. Two English captains when touring Australia did not appear in a single Test in a series. Name the captains and the series.

10. In two succeeding series all five tosses were won first by the home captain and then by the visiting captain. Name the series.

11. Who are the only captains to win all tosses in a series of at least five matches?

12. Who is the only Scotsman to captain England?

13. Which English captain failed in his bid to enter parliament when he stood as a candidate in Cardiff against the future Prime Minister, James Callaghan?

14. Which Australian captain led his country but never his state?

15. After losing a Test match, and thereby a series in England, which Australian captain was also removed as captain of his club and state, leading him to announce his retirement?

16. Which Australian all-rounder captained his country in only one Test series at the age of 39?
(a) George Giffen (b) Jack Ryder (c) Vic Richardson

17. Who made the first declaration in a Test in Australia?
(a) Herbie Collins (b) Percy Chapman (c) Archie MacLaren

18. Who was the first captain who put his opponents in to bat?

19. Who is the youngest England Test captain?

20. Who is the youngest Australian Test captain?

21. Who was the last Oxbridge captain of England?

22. Who led Australia and England in the 1978-79 series in which World Series Cricket players were unavailable?

23. What was the result of the 1978-79 series?

24. Which English captain is generally regarded as having pioneered slow over-rates?

25. What were the middle names of these Test captains?
(a) Bob Simpson (b) Mike Smith (c) Bill Woodfull
(d) Colin Cowdrey

26. What is the highest score by an English captain in Australia?

27. What is the highest score by an English captain in England?

28. What is the highest score by an Australian captain in Australia?

29. What is the highest score by an Australian captain in England?

30. Who is the only Australian captain to lead four touring sides to England?

31. Which two Australian captains and one English captain led three touring sides to each others' countries?

32. How many players captained Australia in their first Anglo-Australian Test?

33. How many players captained England in their first Anglo-Australian Test?
    (a) 5 (b) 7 (c) 9 (d) 11

34. Which Australian captain was dropped from the side only two matches after he had carried his bat through a Test innings?

35. When English captain Mike Denness dropped himself as captain for the Fourth Test of the 1974-75 series who replaced him as leader?

36. When Australian captain Bob Simpson missed the First and Third Tests of the 1965-66 series with a broken wrist and chicken pox who replaced him as leader?

37. Who was the last English captain to win an Ashes series?

38. Whose sporting declaration in 2001 enabled England to break a Headingley record by scoring 311 runs on the last day to win by six wickets.

39. Who captained England against Don Bradman's Invincibles?

40. Who is the only captain to gain a 5-0 whitewash in a series?

Captain of the English Eleven.
Mr. A. E. R. Gilligan

BATTING

1. Who was the first English batsman to score a Test century against Australia?

2. Which English batsman holds the record for the highest score on his Test debut and what is that score?

3. Who is the only batsman to make centuries in his first three Ashes Tests?

4. Who am I? I remain the fastest scoring batsman of all time but I made just one century for my country.

5. Who is the batsman who made centuries in his first two and last two Ashes Tests?

6. Which batsman made consecutive scores of 99, 98 and 97?

7. In which series did he do this?

8. Who hit the first six in Test cricket?

9. Who am I? I was a punishing opening and middle-order Australian batsman of the 1950s and 1960s who liked to remove the shine from a new ball by clouting it for four? My autobiography, *By Hook or by Cut*, epitomised my play.

10. Who was the only batsman to be dismissed 'handled ball' in Ashes matches?

11. Who scored the first pair in Test cricket?

12. Who was the first Australian to score a pair in Test cricket?

13. Who are the only three batsmen to score more than 800 runs in a Test series?

14. Who are the only three batsmen to score four centuries in a Test series?

15. Who was the first Australian batsman to score three centuries in a Test series?

16. Which three other Australian batsmen scored three centuries in a Test series on more than one occasion?

17. Who was the first English batsman to score three centuries in a Test series?

18. Which English batsman scored three centuries in a Test series on more than one occasion?

19. Which three other English batsmen scored three centuries in a Test series?

20. Who was the first batsman to make 500 runs in a series?

21. Who is the only batsman to score 500 runs in a series without making a century?

22. When Len Hutton reached his monumental score of 364 at The Oval in 1938 who was the first person to shake his hand?

23. Who are the four Australian batsmen to score centuries in each innings of a Test match?

24. Who are the three English batsmen to score centuries in each innings of a Test match?

25. Who were the first Australian and English players to carry their bat through a Test innings?

26. Who were the last Australian and English players to carry their bat through a Test innings?

27. Who is the only batsman to carry his bat through a Test innings on two occasions?

28. Which English batsmen holds the record for the most number of runs in England in a five Test series?

29. Of English batsmen who have scored over 2000 runs in Test matches which two averaged more than 60 runs per innings?

30. What do Roy Minnett, Arthur Richardson and Arthur Chipperfield have in common?

31. What do Charles Bannerman, William Murdoch, Percy McDonnell, Harry Graham and Ian Healy have in common?

32. Which Australian captain's innings of 121 out of 198 at Sydney in 1978-79 represents the highest percentage of runs from the bat by a player making over a century?

33. Who were the Australian opening batsmen who passed England's score of 241 before their partnership was broken at Adelaide Oval in 1965-66?

34. Which Australian batsman hit a huge six on to the top level of the Lord's pavilion during his Man of the Match performance in the Centenary Test of 1980?

35. Who is the only clergyman to open the batting for England?

36. Who is the last English player to make a century on his Ashes debut?

37. Who was the last Englishman to make a double century against Australia?

38. Who was the last Australian to make a double century against England?

39. Which English batsman holds the record for the most number of runs in a Test series in England?

40. Who was the last English batsman to score 500 runs in a series against Australia?

41. Which three Australian batsmen have scored 100 runs before lunch on the first day of a Test match?

42. Which two English batsmen have added 100 runs to their overnight score before lunch in a Test match?

43. What is the only occasion when four batsmen have each made centuries in a Test innings?

44. What was the occasion when three batsmen each made centuries in a Test innings and a fourth was dismissed for 99?

45. Who, aged 46 years and 82 days, is the oldest player to score a Test century?

46. Which current Australian Test batsmen each toured England in 1993 without playing a Test?

47. Which Australian middle-order batsman of the 1980s and 1990s averaged 88 on his only English tour?

48. What is the most runs scored in a day in a Test match? (a) 420 (b) 451 (c) 475 (d) 502

49. Who scored it?

50. What is the only occasion when both teams scored more than 600 runs in their first innings?

Clarrie Grimmett

BOWLING

1. Which English fast bowler published several books of poetry?
   (a) Harold Larwood (b) Fred Trueman (c) John Snow
   (d) Bob Willis

2. Which Australian fast bowler was employed as a night-soil carter?

3. Who delivered two consecutive overs in a Test match?

4. The 'bosey' is an alternative name for the googly or wrong'un, and was named after its inventor who first employed it during the 1903-04 series in Australia. What was his name?

5. Who is the only Australian bowler to concede 200 runs in a Test innings? When and where?

6. Who is the only English bowler to concede 200 runs in a Test innings? When and where?

7. 'Ranji' was the diminutive for the Indian born English Test batsman Kumar Shri Ranjitsinhji but it was also the nickname for an Australian slow bowler. Who was he?

8. Which Australian left-arm pace bowler was often beset by injuries but captured 27 wickets at 16 in four Tests of the 1990-91 series, including 13 for 148 in the Second Test at Melbourne?

9. When Jim Laker took 19 wickets for 90 runs at Old Trafford in 1956 who took the other wicket, and whom did he dismiss?

10. Which spin bowler for Australia invented the 'flipper'?

11. Which 1960s Australian fast bowler reduced his speed mid-career to concentrate on cut and swing, and employ a 'knuckle ball' derived from baseball as a deceptive change of pace?

12. Who was the first bowler to take ten wickets in a Test?

13. Who was the first bowler to have 100 runs scored from his bowling in an innings?

14. Who was the first bowler to have 100 runs scored from his bowling in an innings without obtaining a wicket?

15. Who was the last Australian bowler to take ten wickets in a Test?

16. Who was the last English bowler to take ten wickets in a Test?

17. Who are the only two Australian bowlers to take 10 wickets on debut in a Test?

18. What is the best performance in an innings by a bowler in his Test debut?

19. Who are the two English bowlers to take 10 wickets on their Test debut?

20. Who were the last Australian and English bowlers to take a Test hat-trick?

21. What is the record number of wickets by an Australian bowler in a five Test series?

22. Of the 20 English and Australian bowlers to take 100 wickets in Test matches which two have done so at an average of less than 20 runs per wicket?

23. Who is the only bowler to take two hat-tricks in Test matches?

24. Who took the first Test hat-trick?

25. Which Australian left-arm wrist-spinner of the 1950s and 1960s employed a characteristic 'kangaroo hop' in his bowling stride?

26. Who are the only three left-arm bowlers to take 30 wickets in a series?

27. Of English bowlers who have taken 100 wickets against Australia who has the best wicket average per match? (a) Sydney Barnes (b) Alec Bedser (c) Wilfred Rhodes (d) Ian Botham

28. Of Australian bowlers who have taken 100 wickets against England who has the best wicket average per match? (a) Bill O'Reilly (b) Charlie Turner (c) Ray Lindwall (d) Dennis Lillee

29. Who bowled the most balls in a Test match?

30. Who bowled the most balls in a Test innings?

31. Who is the only English bowler to have taken 10 wickets in a match on four occasions?

32. Two Australian bowlers have taken 10 wickets in a match four times. Who are they?

33. Who are the leading bowlers for Australia and England in Test matches?

34. Which English and Australian bowlers hold the record for the most wickets in a Test series in England?

35. Who is the only bowler to take more than 40 wickets in a series on two occasions?

36. Which Australian and English bowlers hold the record for the most wickets in a Test series in Australia?

37. Who is the only bowler to concede 300 runs in a Test match?

38. What is the only time eleven bowlers were used in an innings?

39. Which Australian spin bowlers were known as 'the millionaire' and 'the miser'?

40. Who was the Australian fast-medium bowler who was said to have to have withdrawn from the first Test in 1877 because he preferred to attend the Warrnambool Show?

Keith Miller

ALL-ROUNDERS

1. Who are the only two players to make a century and take five wickets in an innings in a Test match?

2. Which doughty 42-year-old Australian Test all-rounder's career ended following food poisoning in the Brisbane Test of 1928-29?

3. Which all-rounder holds first and last wicket partnership records for England?

4. Who is the only all-rounder to score 400 runs and take more than 30 wickets in a series?

5. Who scored more than 200 runs and took eight wickets in a match and ended up on the losing side?

6. Who is the only English all-rounder to score 250 runs and take 30 wickets in a series? Name the two occasions he did so.

7. Who are the only two Australian all-rounders to achieve the double of 1000 runs and 100 Test wickets?

8. Who are the only two English all-rounders to achieve the double of 1000 runs and 100 Test wickets?

9. Which batsman scored three centuries in a Test series seventeen years after he had taken 11 wickets in a Test match as a left-arm spin bowler?

10. Two Australian all-rounders would have been regarded as only promising in their first five years of Test cricket in the early 1950s but became dominant performers late in that decade and into the 1960s. Who were they?

Ian Healy

WICKET-KEEPERS

1. Which wicket-keepers have captained their country in Ashes matches?

2. Which English wicket-keeper discarded his pads and took 4 wickets for 19 runs bowling underarm lobs?

3. When Bert Oldfield was injured in the Third Test of the Bodyline series who was his replacement for the next match?

4. Who was the English wicket-keeper with only a moderate batting record who was surprisingly selected as a batsman in the First Test of the 1950-51 series?

5. Which Australian wicket-keeper was employed as an undertaker?

6. Which former English wicket-keeper subsequently acted as scorer and baggage man for Peter May's 1958-59 touring side to Australia?

7. Who has recorded the most stumpings by an Australian and an English wicket-keeper?

8. Which Australian wicket-keeper of the 1930s was subsequently a prisoner of the Japanese at Changi in the Second World War, returned to the Victorian side briefly after the war, and played several first-class games in England as late as 1961?

9. Who was the first Australian wicket-keeper to score a century against England in a Test match, and in which game did this occur?

10. Two other Australian wicket-keepers have scored centuries in Ashes Tests. Who are they?

11. Which four English wicket-keepers have scored centuries in Ashes Tests?

12. Which Australian cricketer was chosen as the reserve wicket-keeper on the 1890 tour of England but had never previously kept wickets in his life?

13. Which wicket-keeper made nine dismissals in the Lord's Test of 1956, Australia's only win of that series?

14. Which Australian wicket-keeper toured England twice in 1930 and 1938 but never played in a Test match?

15. Who was the Australian wicket-keeper (and leg-spinner) who lead his team's bowling averages with 12 wickets at 20.83 on the 1993 English tour?

16. Which Australian wicket-keeper holds the record of 28 dismissals in a series? (a) Don Tallon (b) Wally Grout (c) Rod Marsh (d) Ian Healy

17. Who is the only English wicket-keeper to tour Australia five times?

18. Which English wicket-keeper who toured Australia in 1978-79 later died by his own hand?

19. Who was the Australian wicket-keeper of the mid-1980s who began his Test career as an opening batsman?

20. Who is the English wicket-keeper to make 100 centuries in first-class cricket?

TWELFTH MEN

1. Australia appointed the first twelfth man in a Test match. Who was he?
   (a) John Edwards (b) Edward Johns (c) John Smith

2. In what match did this initial twelfth man appointment occur?

3. Who was the twelfth man in the First Test of the 1901-02 series in Sydney who later invented a backhand stroke in tennis named after him, and represented Australia in the Davis Cup in 1907?

4. Who was twelfth man for Australia in the Second Test of the 1928-29 series in Melbourne?

5. Who was the batsman who was Australian twelfth man in the first two Tests of the 1946-47 series when Arthur Morris failed with scores of 2 and 5 in his team's innings victories but then saw Morris recover in the Third and Fourth Tests to make three centuries in successive innings?
   (a) Ken Meuleman (b) Bill Brown (c) Ron Hamence
   (d) Phil Ridings

6. Which later Minister for Defence was twelfth man for Australia in the Fourth Test of the 1962-63 series at Adelaide Oval?

7. Who, after being dropped to twelfth man, returned to the side in the next Test match and scored a triple-century?

8. Which leg-spinner was in the Australian twelve for all six Tests of the 1974-75 series but played in just two matches and was then omitted from the team which toured England in 1975?

9. What was unusual about Jason Gillespie being twelfth man in his home town of Adelaide in the Third Test of the 1998-99 series?

10. Who were the Australian and English twelfth men for the Centenary Test at Melbourne?

Ernie Jones

CENTENARY TEST

1. Who were the Australian and English captains?

2. How many runs were scored on a full first day's play?
   (a) 167 (b) 267 (c) 367

3. With its first innings score of 138 did Australia lead or trail England by 43 runs?

4. Which Australian middle-order batsman making his Test debut hit Tony Greig for five consecutive fours in his second innings of 56?

5. Who were the umpires in the game?

6. Who in his acceptance speech for the Man of the Match award said: 'thanks for the bump on the back of the head, Dennis'?

7. Which Australian opening batsman had his jaw broken and returned to bat at number ten in the second innings with it wired in place?

8. Which Australian bowler took 11 wickets for 165 runs and then stood down from the English tour which followed?

9. What was the winning margin to Australia?
   (a) 45 runs (b) 3 wickets (c) 80 runs

10. How many former Australian and Engl.sh Test players attended the Test match and associated celebrations?
    (a) 118 (b) 218 (c) 318

David Gower

SCANDALS

1. Who were the players known as the 'Big Six' who withdrew from the 1912 tour of England over a dispute with the Australian Board of Control regarding team management?

2. Who was the player/manager at the centre of the 'Big Six' dispute in 1912?
   (a) Frank Laver (b) Peter McAlister (c) Charles Eady

3. Which two English players indulged in dare-devil flying of a Tiger Moth over Cararra on the Gold Coast during the 1994-95 Ashes tour?

4. The wife of which Australian batsman reputedly dropped her knitting as her husband went out to bat at the Melbourne Cricket Ground, thereby missing his entire Test career?

5. The wife of which Australian player, keeping her own scorecards, disputed the figures kept by the official scorer Bill Ferguson on Fergie's first tour of England in 1905?

6. Who was the Australian all-rounder who took the wicket of Archie MacLaren with his first ball in Test cricket, and later made headlines by suing a Catholic priest for having an affair with his wife?

7. Which English captain became inebriated at an Adelaide vice-regal reception the night before a Test match, crashed his hire car on the way back to his hotel, and thus missed the Test with injury?

8. What office did Clem Jones hold when he sacked the Brisbane Cricket Ground (Woollongabba) curator before the 1970 Test match and then prepared the pitch himself?

9. Who was the English criminal on whose behalf a Test match was sabotaged at Headingley in 1975 by supporters pouring oil on the wicket?
(a) George Davis (b) George Harrison (c) Myra Hindley (d) Ronald Biggs

10. What were the odds on an English win taken up by Rod Marsh and Dennis Lillee in their notorious bet at the Headingley Test in 1981?
(a) 50/1 (b) 100/1 (c) 200/1 (d) 500/1

11. According to Wally Hammond's biographer David Foot, his subject suffered a major disease early in his career, the treatment of which later led to abrupt mood swings. What was the disease?
(a) epilepsy (b) schizophrenia (c) syphilis (d) hepatitis

12. Which Australian fast bowler liked to indulge in nude wrestling with team-mates in the dressing rooms?

13. Which Australian fast bowler often celebrated a wicket by kissing the fieldsman who took the catch?

14. What commercial publicity stunt during the Perth Test of December 1979 provoked a protest by English captain Mike Brearley and a tantrum by the batsman Dennis Lillee?

15. Which English captain led his team from the Sydney Cricket Ground as a protest against crowd violence after his fast bowler had been molested by spectators?

16. Which English opening batsman protested against his run out dismissal at the Adelaide Oval and threw his bat away in a display of petulance?

17. What action by Don Bradman created a storm when a photograph was published of him walking in conversation with King George VI at Balmoral in 1948?

18. Which Australian batsman read of his selection in the 1890 touring side to England only to learn that a mistake had been made and the man chosen was his brother-in-law, Syd Gregory?

19. Who was the Australian batsman who outraged officialdom by jumping a turnstile at the Melbourne Cricket Ground in 1946-47 because he had forgotten his player's pass and was due to bat?

20. Who was the Australian pace bowler who dislocated his bowling shoulder and ruptured nerves in his upper arm while tackling a spectator who invaded the field during the First Test at Perth on 13 November 1982?

21. When champion leg-spinner Clarrie Grimmett was omitted from the Australian Test sides of 1936-37 and 1938 who was his replacement?

22. Who was the English wicket-keeper forced to miss the first-ever Test match in 1877 because he was awaiting trial in New Zealand?

23. An Australian batsman and an English bowler came to blows following the First Test at Sydney in 1886-87 which England won by 13 runs. The bowler, who had taken 6-28 in the final innings took a huge swipe at his adversary's face and succeeded only in smashing his fist against a wall. Who were the players?

24. When Michael Atherton closed England's second innings at Sydney in 1994-95 in an attempt to force a win which batsman remained 98 not out?

25. Which Australian spin bowler was rumoured to have been omitted from the 1930 English tour because of fears about the legitimacy of his action?
(a) Don Blackie (b) Bert Ironmonger (c) Ron Oxenham

26. Which English spin bowler, who had been no-balled elsewhere in Test cricket, came under scrutiny during the 1958-59 Ashes series in Australia?

27. Which Australian opening bowler created a furore and throwing accusations after taking 6-38 in the Second Test at Melbourne in 1958-59?

28. Who was the curator who ordered the watering of the Melbourne Cricket Ground wicket during the rest day of the Third Test of the 1954-55 series?

29. Which Australian 'batsman' averaged 1.83 from six innings in his three Tests in 1887 and 1891-92 yet toured England in 1893 after pressure was put on selectors by his brother to choose him?

30. Who were the principal antagonists who engaged in fisticuffs at an Australian selection meeting during the 1911-12 series and led eventually to one of them joining the 'Big Six'?

KANGAROO - TAIL SOUP

Chef Bradman "I've been in it twice myself,
dear boys and I know."

FAMILIES

1. What are the initials of the three English brothers who appeared in a Test match together against Australia in 1880?

2. What are the initials of the three Australian brothers who represented their country in Test cricket against England?

3. Two pairs of fathers and sons represented England against Australia. Who were they?

4. Which Australian captain and all-rounder was the son-in-law of Test player Roy Park?

5. Which English all-rounder and Australian batsman are brothers-in-law?

6. Current Australian Test selector Andrew Hilditch's father-in-law was an Australian captain, coach and also a selector. Who is he?

7. When Mark Waugh made his Test debut at Adelaide Oval in 1991 whom did he replace in the Australian side?

8. Who are the Australian brother and sister combination to appear in Test matches against England?

9. Who am I? I was an English-born Australian leg-spinner who appeared briefly in Test cricket in the 1880s, was later an Australian lawn bowls champion, and the great-grandfather of Australian batsman Paul Sheahan.

10. Who were the last English pair of brothers to appear against Australia in a Test match?

UMPIRES

1. Which Australian umpires were known by the nicknames 'Dimboola Jim' and 'The Chief Justice'?

2. Who is the only Australian umpire to officiate in Test matches and as a field umpire in an interstate football match at the Melbourne Cricket Ground?

3. Which English umpire lost an arm during the First World War and became a leading Test umpire either side of World War II?

4. In the nineteenth century cricketers sometimes alternated between playing and umpiring. Name the two Australians who umpired in Test matches before appearing for their country as players?

5. Which Australian Test batting hero umpired 12 Test matches from 1887-88 to 1901-02 after his playing days had ended?

6. A mistaken run out decision involving substitute Jim Burke running for Colin McDonald in the Adelaide Test of 1958-59 led which umpire to retire from cricket after the game?

7. Who was the Australian umpire who cautioned John Snow for intimidatory bowling after he felled Terry Jenner with a bouncer in the final Sydney Test of 1970-71?

8. Who is the most recent English Test player to officiate in Tests as an umpire?

9. Who is the only bowler to be no-balled for throwing in a Test match?

10. Who was the umpire who made the first call and in which match did it occur?

W. G. Grace, 1880

GENERAL

1. Which Olympic gold medal winning heavyweight boxer captained England in two Test series in Australia?

2. Who was the last double international sportsman for England and what was his other sport?

3. Who was the pace bowler for England in the 1990s who played league football in South Australia for North Adelaide?

4. Who was the Australian opening batsman who subsequently managed a rebel tour of South Africa, defended the tour in a book he wrote: *'Guilty': Bob Hawke or Kim Hughes?* and was an unsuccessful Liberal candidate at the 1993 federal election?
(a) Bruce Francis (b) Alan Turner (c) Graeme Watson

5. Which English side described at the time of selection as the 'best ever' to tour Australia ended up losing the five Test series 0-4?

6. How many times did England win an Ashes Test match at Lord's during the twentieth century?

7. Which Sydney born and raised all-rounder represented Australia in three Tests in 1888 but never played first-class cricket in his home country.

8. Which Australian opening batsman, who scored 207 in the Brisbane Test of 1970-71, had earlier in his career been sponsored by Sir Robert Menzies for specialised coaching by Clarrie Grimmett to assist his leg-spin bowling?

9. Who are the three New Zealand-born Australian Test cricketers.

10. When and where was the last occasion when a horse was used to operate the rolling of a Test pitch in Australia?

11. What was the name of the horse?
(a) Francis (b) Mr Ed (c) Dobbin

12. Who was the first Australian batsman described as the 'Second Bradman'?

13. When was the last Australian tour of England which travelled by ship?

14. Which 21-year-old English all-rounder took 30 wickets in his only Test series against Australia?

15. Who was the best known Brylcream boy?

16. Which Australian batsman and cricket writer of the same name are often confused?

17. The following Australian Test cricketers—Joe Darling, Sam Loxton, Gil Langley, Tom Veivers—all had a second career in common. What was it?

18. Complete the number series 165, ___, ___, 334?

19. Complete the number series 63, 152, ___, ___, 364?

20. Which Australian batsman was described by his biographer as 'The Keats of Cricket'?

21. Len Pascoe changed his name by deed poll. What was his original family name?

22. What was the name of the legendary spectator of the Sydney Hill known as 'Yabba'?

23. Which Australian spin bowler was notorious for his mutterings of 'c'mon South Melbourne' when in the field on English tours?

24. In which two Ashes series in Australia between the First and Second World Wars were six ball overs used?

25. All Test matches in Australia were played out until 1946-47 except for one summer when two draws were recorded. When and where did the draws take place?

26. When Keith Miller resumed his innings at Adelaide Oval in 1947 and hit the first ball of the day over the fence for six. Who was the bowler who delivered the ball?
(a) Alec Bedser (b) Bill Edrich (c) Doug Wright
(d) Norman Yardley

27. What tag did Jack Badcock, Ian Craig, Norm O'Neill and Doug Walters share?

28. Name the four English cricketing knights.

29. When Doug Walters hit the last ball of the day for six to bring up his century in a session at the Perth Test of 1974 who was the offending bowler?
(a) Chris Old (b) Bob Willis (c) Geoff Arnold
(d) Tony Greig

30. In what series did the Australian players wear baggy green caps for the first time?

31. In what series did the Australian team first wear the green and gold colours?

32. What was the first and last English tour to operate under the control of the Marylebone Cricket Club?

33. Who had the longest career span for an English player in Ashes matches?

34. Who had the longest career span for an Australian player in Ashes matches?

35. When was the last series of timeless Tests in Australia?

36. Which English player was on the losing side in seven consecutive Ashes series?

37. Which Australian player was on the winning side in the same seven consecutive series?

38. In which city was the first ball-by-ball cricket broadcast made during the 1924-25 series?
(a) Sydney (b) Melbourne (c) Adelaide

39. What historic event provided a substitute for the abandoned Melbourne Test of 1970-71

40. Which English comedian invented the character of a fearsome female fast bowler, Lillian Thomson, following the destruction wrought by Dennis Lillee and Jeff Thomson in the 1974-75 series?
(a) Peter Cook (b) Spike Milligan (c) Richard Stilgoe
(d) John Cleese

41. Which titled aristocrats managed English Test teams to Australia?

42. When was the last series with eight ball overs?

43. Who as thirteenth man took a magnificent catch which changed the course of a 1930 Test match in England's favour.

44. What is the only time a team has been unchanged throughout a five Test series?

45. What is the greatest number of players used by Australia in a five Test series?

46. What is the greatest number of players used by England in a five Test series?

47. Which two Australian players with the same surname made their debuts for the same state and their country together?

48. Which Australian captain previously represented his country in hockey at the 1956 Melbourne Olympics?

49. Which leading Australian legal and political figure wrote an essay on Don Bradman in *Wisden*?

50. Which Australian Invincible usually 'signed' his name with a rubber stamp?

Denis Compton
Adelaide Test, 1951

England captain Lionel Tennyson tosses the coin
for Australia's Warwick Armstrong at The Oval, 1921.

GOOD BEGINNINGS, BAD STARTS, BAD ENDINGS

1. Who is the only player to make 300 runs in his first Test match?

2. Which two players made 200 runs in their Test debuts for Australia?

3. Who is the only player, who made a century on his Ashes debut, to die by his own hand?

4. Which Australian batsman, who made a century on debut, died in a New Zealand mental asylum in 1907 following years of alcoholism?

5. Which stylish Australian opening batsman succumbed to alcoholism and the life of a derelict before dying of a heart attack at 33?

6. Which ailment caused the early death of Victor Trumper at 38? (a) Grave's Disease (b) Pneumonia (c) Leukemia (d) Bright's Disease

7. Who was the Australian and English Test all-rounder who shot himself in his rented room and left his entire estate of £4 to his landlady?

8. Which fast bowler who as a stretcher-bearer in Palestine was the only Australian Test cricketer to lose his life in the First World War?

9. Which two batsmen who each made 100 first-class centuries began their Test careers by bagging a pair of ducks on debut?

10. Which other 100 century batsman began his Test career with a duck?

Don Bradman

DON BRADMAN

1. What was Don Bradman's score in the 1946 Brisbane Test match when the disputed catch by Jack Ikin was disallowed? What was his eventual score when he was dismissed?

2. How many record partnerships for Australia does Bradman hold?

3. Name the partnerships and how many runs they comprised.

4. Where did Bradman make his Test debut?

5. What were his scores in his first Test?

6. An English bowler, who dismissed Bradman during the game, described him as his rabbit? Who made this injudicious remark?

7. What record did Bradman set in his second Test match?

8. What innings did Bradman generally rate as his best in Test cricket?

9. As a bowler Bradman dismissed one English batsman. Who was he?

10. In the home of which English player did Bradman spend time recuperating from his illness and an operation at the end of the 1934 English tour?

11. Bradman made five ducks in Ashes Tests? Who were the bowlers who dismissed him?

12. Which ball did Bradman say was the best that ever took his wicket?

13. On his last English tour a leg trap was employed against Bradman in order to dismiss him. Who was the bowler and fielder successful on three occasions with this attack.

14. After his dismissal at The Oval for a duck in his final Test innings in 1948 what did he say after returning to the pavilion?
(a) 'Fancy doing that' (b) 'Jeez! Some days you can be stiff' (c) 'Such is life'

15. Who filmed the same final Test innings from the dressing room and when he returned reportedly said, "I got your entire innings, Don"

16. Bradman hit 5028 runs against England. The first six he struck came in the Bodyline Test in Adelaide in his twelfth Test. Who was the bowler who was lifted over the boundary?

17. Who wrote the song, *Our Don Bradman*?

18. What was Bradman's Test average against England?
(a) 99.94 (b) 95.14 (c) 89.78

19. Bradman's entire Test cricket was played on Australian and English grounds. How many grounds did he play on? What were they?

20. What batting statistic do Bradman and England's Trevor Bailey share as Test batsmen?

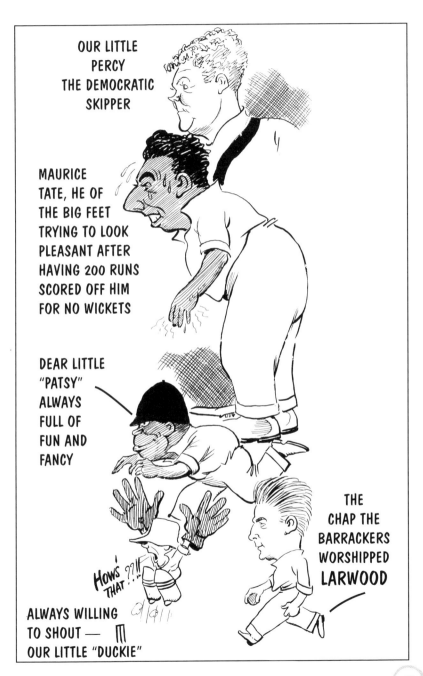

BODYLINE

1. Which Australian journalist is usually credited with creating the term 'bodyline' as part of a space-saving measure in a cable message to his newspaper?
(a) Hugh Buggy (b) Jack Worrall (c) Johnny Moyes
(d) Jack Fingleton

2. Which combination of college (English public school) and university did English captain Douglas Jardine attend?
(a) Eton/Oxford, (b) Harrow/Cambride,
(c) Eton/Cambridge, (d) Winchester/Oxford

3. Which English pace bowler and leg theorist is often implicated in planning Bodyline as a form of attack?

4. Australian captain Bill Woodfull was a teacher at which Victorian educational institution?
(a) Melbourne High School (b) Melbourne Grammar
(c) University of Melbourne

5. Apart from Jardine there were four other amateurs in the 1932-33 English touring side. Who were they?

6. Who was the English batsman dropped from the side, only one match after he had made a century on debut, because of his opposition to Bodyline?

7. Who were the five England pace bowlers in the 1932-33 English touring side?

8. Why can three of these pace bowlers be discounted when Bodyline is discussed?

9. Whose brilliant innings of 187 not out in the First Test at Sydney almost strangled Bodyline at birth?

10. What role did Bernhardt Tobin play in the Bodyline series?
    (a) groundsman at the Sydney Cricket Ground
    (b) ground announcer at the Melbourne Cricket Ground
    (c) twelfth man for Australia in the Fourth Test at Brisbane

11. Who were the two English managers on the Bodyline tour?

12. Who was the Aboriginal fast bowler promoted as capable of retaliating with Bodyline if Australia had chosen to answer fire with fire?

13. What was Don Bradman's batting average during the Bodyline series? (a) 56 (b) 64 (c) 70 (d) 99

14. How many wickets at what average did Harold Larwood take his wickets during the Bodyline series?
    (a) 20 wickets at 27 (b) 26 wickets at 24 (c) 33 wickets at 19 (d) 38 wickets at 14

15. Which former Australian Prime Minister was given a diplomatic role to smooth tempers between the Australian Board of Control and the Marylebone Cricket Club after the telegram exchange?
    (a) Alfred Deakin (b) Billy Hughes (c) Stanley Bruce
    (d) Robert Menzies

16. Who said of Douglas Jardine, 'He might win us the Ashes and lose us an Empire'?

17. Who were the actors who played the roles of Don Bradman, Douglas Jardine and Harold Larwood in the 1980s mini-series, Bodyline?

18. Who was the scorer for Jardine's MCC team?

19. Which Australian opening bowler between the Fourth and Fifth Tests became the first player to take 10 wickets in an innings of a Sheffield Shield match?

20. Who were the umpires who stood in each of the Bodyline Tests?

GROUNDS

1. What ground staged the first Test match in England?

2. Who are the Australian cricketers whose names are commemorated on grandstands at the Sydney Cricket Ground?

3. Which grounds in England and Australia have each been the venue for just one Test?

4. The following thoroughfares—Kirkstall Lane, Vulture Street, Brunton Avenue, Vauxhall Road—are adjacent to which grounds?

5. At which two grounds are the members grandstands side-on to the wicket?

6. Where is Father Time?

7. By what name is the northern end of Adelaide Oval commonly known?

8. With which grounds are the following curators associated?
   (a) Bert Flack (b) Athol Watkins (c) Mick Hunt
   (d) Les Burdett

9. At which ground did England record its greatest innings score of 7-903d against Australia?

10. At which ground did Australia record its greatest innings score of 6-729d against England?

11. At which ground did England record its smallest innings score of 45 against Australia?

12. At which ground did Australia record its smallest innings score of 36 against England?

13. At which ground was the highest match aggregate of 1753 runs achieved?

14. At which ground did a Test match run for eight days?

15. The Oval in 1938 saw England defeat Australia by its greatest winning innings and runs margin. What was the margin? (a) Innings and 579 runs (b) Innings and 487 runs (c) Innings and 358 runs

16. The very next Test between the sides at Brisbane in 1946 saw Australia avenge this defeat with its own largest win by an innings and runs. What was its margin?
(a) Innings and 425 runs (b) Innings and 332 runs
(c) Innings and 287 runs

17. The series was 1928-29 and England gained its greatest ever win over Australia by a runs margin (675) at a ground which staged its only Test. What was the ground?

18. When Australia defeated England by a record 562 runs in 1934 at which ground did it achieve this result?

19. With what ground was the 'ridge' associated?

20. What is the 'Fremantle Doctor'?

21. On which ground staging its first Test match was there a dust-storm so violent that the players were forced to lie down flat to avoid suffocation?

22. On which ground was the lowest match aggregate of 291 runs for 40 wickets recorded?

23. What is the shortest Test match?

24. 1723 is the most runs for a Test match in England. Where was it? (a) Headingley 1948 (b) Lord's 1930 (c) Trent Bridge 1938

25. England defeated Australia twice by one wicket margins. When and where did these wins occur?

26. England and Australia each defeated the other by a 3 run margins. When and where did these matches occur?

27. On which ground was a hill known as 'The Hill'?

28. With which ground is Bay 13 associated?

29. Which Australian ground staged its first Test match in 1970?

30. At which ground in 1993 did Shane Warne deliver what has been described as 'the ball of the century'?

Invincibles 1948

INVINCIBLES

1. How many runs did Australia score against Essex in a single day's play?
   (a) 550 (b) 645 (c) 721

2. What did Essex achieve that no other side was able to do on the 1948 tour?

3. Who was the leading run scorer for Australia during the 1948 series?
   (a) Don Bradman (b) Arthur Morris (c) Lindsay Hassett
   (d) Sid Barnes

4. Who took the most wickets for Australia during the 1948 series?

5. Which Australian short-leg fielder was struck a sickening blow in the ribs at Old Trafford by England tailender Dick Pollard, causing him to miss three weeks of cricket?

6. Who was the English batsman who replaced Len Hutton for the Fourth Test at Headingley and quickly sank without trace?

7. Who as reserve wicket-keeper replaced the injured Don Tallon in the Headingley Test?

8. Name the English off-spinner who took 0 for 93 on the last day at Headingley in 1948 as Australia posted its greatest fourth innings victory target of 3-404?

9. Solemnity surrounding Don Bradman's duck in The Oval Test has tended to overshadow superb performances by Arthur Morris and Ray Lindwall during the game. What did they achieve?

10. Who were the two Invincibles/Invisibles not to appear in a Test match during the 1948 Tour?

Australian opener Arthur Morris

ONE TEST WONDERS

1. Which 1930s Australian batsman was known as the 'Second Kippax'?

2. Which Australian bowler, labelled a 'thrower', made his only Test appearance in the 1958-59 Test series?

3. Which Australian all-rounder's sole appearance in the final Test match at The Oval in 1997 occurred when he was called up from county cricket with Gloucestershire to replace injured players?

4. I am one of only three players to take 10 wickets in an innings in the Sheffield Shield. I opened the bowling for my state and in the First Test at Brisbane in the 1965-66 series. Who am I?
   (a) Peter Allan (b) Ian Brayshaw (c) Colin Guest

5. We were English middle-order batsmen who each played club cricket in Adelaide as part of our development. One of us played his only Test at at The Oval in 1981 and the other at Adelaide Oval in 1986-87? Who are we?

6. Which father of a recent English Test cricketer played his sole game for England at Trent Bridge in 1985 as well as representing Manchester United at football?

7. Which Australian pace bowler took 5-63 and 1-14 in his only Test match at The Oval in 1977?

8. Who was the Australian fast-medium bowler who replaced Ray Lindwall for the Second Test in Melbourne in 1946-47, took three wickets at moderate cost, batted usefully but after being twelfth man in the next two Tests was never called on again?

9. I was a Derbyshire opening bowler who took five wickets in an innings on debut in the Third Test at Leeds in 1905. Who am I?

10. Which batsman, who was the oldest of four brothers to play first-class cricket, replaced Sid Barnes as an opener for the Adelaide Test of 1946-47.

Jack Hobbs, Herbert Sutcliffe

YOUNG AND OLD

1. Who is the youngest Australian player in Test matches?

2. How many teenagers have represented Australia in Test matches?
   (a) 5 (b) 9 (c) 13 (d) 16

3. Who is the oldest English player in Test matches?

4. Who is the oldest Australian player in Test matches?

5. Who scored the most Test centuries after the age of 40?

6. Who are the only teenage batsmen to record centuries in Ashes Tests?

7. Who are the only two teenage bowlers to capture five wickets in an innings in a Test?

8. How many teenagers have represented England in Ashes Test matches?
   (a) 1 (b) 5 (c) 10

9. Which Australian batsman was aged 37 years and 351 days when he made his first and only Test century?

10. Who was the Australian wicket-keeper who was 43 years old on his last tour of England in 1921?

Sailing to England 1938 Jack Badcock (front)
professional dancing champion (left), Sid Barnes (right)

ON TOUR

1. Who was the first Australian batsman to make 2000 first-class runs on an English tour?

2. Which Australian bowler was the first to take 100 first-class wickets on an English tour?

3. Who are the only two Australian bowlers to take 200 first-class wickets on an English tour?

4. Who was the last Australian bowler to take 100 wickets on an English tour?

5. Who was the last Australian batsman to make 2000 runs on an English tour?

6. Who are the three Australian batsmen to average over 100 on an English tour?

7. Who is the only batsman to go through an English tour without scoring a run.

8. Who are the four Australian batsmen to score triple-centuries during an English tour?

9. Who are the two English batsmen to score triple-centuries during an Australian tour?

10. Who are the only two Australian batsmen to score 2500 runs on an English tour?

11. Two of the following four Australian batsmen scored more than 2000 runs on an English tour at least three times. Who are they?
(a) Don Bradman (b) Bill Ponsford (c) Warren Bardsley (d) Neil Harvey

12. Which Australian fast bowler made a disastrous start to the 1938 English tour by being no-balled 19 times for overstepping the crease in his first three overs in the opening match at Worcester?

13. Who was the first English bowler to take 50 wickets on an Australian tour?

14. What was unique about the composition of the English side which played Australia at the Sydney Test of 1887-88?

15. Who was the first batsman for England to make 1000 runs on an Australian tour?

16. Who took the most number of wickets on an Australian tour?

17. Who is the only English batsman to score 1000 runs on three consecutive Australian tours?
(a) Jack Hobbs (b) Patsy Hendren (c) Wally Hammond (d) Len Hutton

18. Who was the last English bowler to take 50 wickets on an Australian tour?

19. Who are the only two English batsmen to score 1500 runs on an Australian tour?

20. Who was the last English batsman to score 1000 runs on an Australian tour?

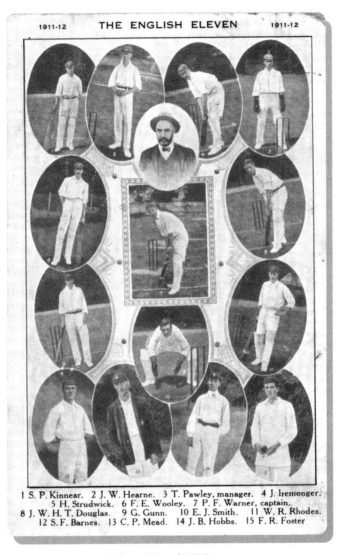

1 S. P. Kinnear.   2 J. W. Hearne.   3 T. Pawley, manager.   4 J. Iremonger.
5 H. Strudwick.   6 F. E. Wooley.   7 P. F. Warner, captain.
8 J. W. H. T. Douglas.   9 G. Gunn.   10 E. J. Smith.   11 W. R. Rhodes.
12 S. F. Barnes.   13 C. P. Mead.   14 J. B. Hobbs.   15 F. R. Foster

Pelham Warner's MCC team
which won the Ashes in 1911-12

ODD SELECTIONS/NON-SELECTIONS

1. Which Australian off-spinner was plucked from Sydney grade cricket to play in the Fifth Test against England in 1986-87 at the Sydney Cricket Ground and then took eight wickets in his Test debut?

2. Who was the 26-year-old Australian medium-fast bowler who took 5-37 in England's first innings, and scored 41 and 11 in last-wicket stands of 81 and 64 at Adelaide Oval in the Third Test of the 1894-95 series, but was then dropped from the side and never reappeared in Test cricket?

3. Who was the English spin bowler who was withdrawn from the English touring party in 1958-59 after he criticised his county captain and team-mates in newspaper articles?

4. Whose omission from the 1896 Australian touring side to England caused the player to switch his allegiance to Middlesex and English cricket where he went on to take more first-class wickets than any other Australian bowler?

5. Which 22-year-old Australian pace bowler was recruited from English league cricket into the Test side for the last two Tests of the 1981 series when the touring side was plagued with injuries?

6. Who was the 35-year-old Victorian left-hand opening batsman who made his Test debut by replacing 34-year-old Victorian left-hand opening batsman Bill Lawry in the Australian side for the Seventh Test of the 1970-71 series?

7. Who was the 20-year-old Australian all-rounder chosen in the Fourth Test of the Bodyline series on the basis of one first-class innings for Victoria during the summer?

8. Who am I? I was a Gloucestershire left-arm orthodox spinner who took 3278 wickets in my first-class career but made my only Test appearance at Old Trafford in 1921?

9. Which English fast bowler who took 11 for 88 in his side's win at Headingley in 1961 was dropped two Tests later at The Oval?

10. Which 41-year-old English batsman was flown to Australia in 1974-75 and rushed straight into the Test team against Dennis Lillee and Jeff Thomson on the world's fastest wicket at Perth?

Colin Cowdrey

NICK AND OTHER NAMES

1. Match the following:

Terror	Pelham Warner
Monkey	Leslie Fleetwood-Smith
Stork	David Gower
Plum	Wally Grout
Chuck	Derek Randall
Noddy	Wayne Phillips
Griz	Geoff Pullar
Arkle	Charles Turner
Flipper	A.N. Hornby
Biggles	Hunter Hendry

2. Match the following:

Lord Ted	Neil Harvey
Nugget	Reggie Foster
Tich	Bill Lawry
Phantom	Henry Scott
Chub	Graeme Corling
Ninna	Ted Dexter
Dusty	A.P. Freeman
Tup	Keith Miller
Tip	Geoff Miller
Sledge	Fred and Maurice Tate

3. What nicknames did the initials of English Test players J.W.H.T. Douglas and P.G.H. Fender provide?

4. Match the following:

Deadly	Gary Gilmour, Angus Fraser
Mary Ann	George Allen
Nobby	Monty Noble
Claw	Rod Marsh
Ollie	Harold Larwood

Tiger	Colin Milburn
Lol	Derek Underwood
Iron Gloves	Bill O'Reilly, E.J. Smith
Gubby	Edward Clarke
Gus	Alan Davidson

5. Match the following:

Gnome	Frank Tyson
Tangles	Ken Mackay
Farmer	Keith Fletcher, Clarrie Grimmett
Skull	Jason Gillespie
Horse	Brian Statham
Tibby	Max Walker
George	Jack White
Slasher	Kerry O'Keefe
Typhoon	Geoff Arnold
Dizzy	Albert Cotter

6. Match the following:

Barnacle	Darren Lehmann
Big Jake	Herbert Collins
Beefy	Kumar Shri Ranjitsinhji
Horseshoe	Steve Waugh
Smith	Bert Ironmonger
Dainty	Elias Hendren
Patsy	David Lloyd
Boof	Jack Iverson
Mumbles	Trevor Bailey
Tugga	Ian Botham

7. Match the following:

Greatheart	Greg Matthews
Junior	Johnny Gleeson
Rowdy	Terry Alderman
Affie	Graham McKenzie
Punter	Lindsay Kline
Garth	Mark Waugh

Clem   Percy McDonnell
Spinner   Ashley Mallett
Mo   Arthur Jarvis
Cho   Ricky Ponting

8. Which players were known as 'The Champion', 'The Coroner', 'The Croucher', 'The Master', 'The Iron Duke', 'The Demon', The Australian Hercules', 'The Big Ship', 'The Guardsman' and 'The Don'?

9. A number of Australian players have not used their first given name. Fill in the gaps:
C _ _ _ _ _ _ L _ _ _ _ _ _ 'Jack' Badcock
E _ _ _ _ J _ _ _ _ Kenneth Burn
W _ _ _ _ _ _ M _ _ _ _ _ _ 'Rick' Darling
J _ _ _ Ross Frederick Duncan
D _ _ _ _ _ R _ _ _ _ _ _ Algernon Gehrs
A _ _ _ _ _ T _ _ _ _ _ _ _ Wallace Grout
M _ _ _ _ _ _ J _ _ _ _ _ 'Roger' Hartigan
R _ _ _ _ _ Neil Harvey
A _ _ _ _ _ Lindsay Hassett
R _ _ _ _ _ John Inverarity
W _ _ _ _ _ _ Albert Stanley Oldfield
A _ _ _ _ _ Paul Sheahan
H _ _ _ _ _ Brian Taber
G _ _ _ _ _ Henry Stevens Trott
J _ _ _ William Trumble
T _ _ _ _ _ W _ _ _ _ _ _ _ 'Tim' Wall
K _ _ _ _ Douglas Walters

10. Some English players are called by other than their first given names. Fill the gaps:
J _ _ _ Michael Brearley
A _ _ _ _ _ Percy Frank Chapman
M _ _ _ _ _ _ Colin Cowdrey
H _ _ _ _ _ E _ _ _ _ 'Tom' Dollery
T _ _ _ _ _ Godfrey Evans

G _ _ _ _ _ Frederick Grace
E _ _ _ _ H _ _ _ _ 'Patsy' Hendren
W _ _ _ _ _ _ Eric Hollies
F _ _ _ _ _ _ _ Stanley Jackson
G _ _ _ _ _ Anthony Richard Lock
C _ _ _ _ _ _ Philip Mead
R _ _ _ _ _ Walter Vivian Robins
J _ _ _ Brian Statham

Neil Harvey

WHO AM I?

1. Who am I? My batting was described by Johnny Moyes as founded on 'doggedness, courage and perseverance' but I later revealed more elegance at the typewriter and became one of the most important writers on the game.

2. Who am I? I was the first English-born Test cricketer to play for Australia since the Second World War. Before doing so I also represented my adopted country as a national serviceman in Vietnam.

3. I was a fast bowler with an open chested action but possessed both a devastating yorker and bouncer. Originally flown to Australia at 21 to replace an injured team-mate I later proved a regular match-winner and captained my country. Who am I?

4. Who am I? I was an Australian opening batsman with a penchant for audacious hook strokes and dazzling but risky running. I played 14 Tests during the World Series Cricket crisis and was once the victim of a Bob Willis bouncer which struck me in the chest and caused me to stop breathing when chewing gum lodged in my throat. A great uncle was an Australian Test captain.

5. Who am I? I was an outstanding schoolboy batsman who had only a modest record for New South Wales before playing my only Test match at Sydney in 1886-87. Although I scored 14 and 30 in a low scoring game I dropped out of first-class cricket the following season before going on to become a senior partner in leading Sydney law firm. A nephew was later an England captain.

6. Who are we? We were both fast-medium bowlers and hard-hitting lower order batsman who played for the same district club as well as our state and Australia, and toured England together on one occasion. We also represented the same Australian Rules league football club at full-forward and each played for our state in that sport.

7. Who am I? I was an Australian fast bowler of the 1980s, born in Wagga Wagga, who balanced a successful Test career with my profession as an optometrist. Since retirement I have coached my state and provided astute comments as a writer and broadcaster.

8. I made centuries in my first and last first-class games over a fifteen year span but played just three Test matches just after the Second World War, including one against England. My greatest claim to fame was touring England as a member of Bradman's Invincibles in 1948.

9. At 37 years of age I made my only appearance for England as right-arm leg spinner, I took 7 wickets for 282 runs from 69 overs in the Fifth Test of the 1909 series. What is my name?

10. I took five wickets in the first innings of the first Test match and am the only player to subsequently appear in Test cricket for both Australia and England in matches between the countries. What is my name?

EMIGRANTS

1. Which Australian all-rounder of the 1970s and 1980s who took 5-71 at Sydney in 1986-87, later played and coached in Lancashire while playing occasional first-class games against touring sides in England until the mid-1990s?

2. Which English spin bowler remodelled his action to become a highly successful state captain in Australia in the 1960s?

3. Which former England fast bowler and schoolmaster later won fame in Australia as a commentator, author and coach?

4. Which English fast bowler was sponsored as an immigrant to Australia by one of his opening batting adversaries just after the Second World War?

5. Which Australian all-rounder enjoyed a substantial professional cricket career in England after World War II before graduating to Test cricket as an umpire?

6. Who is the South African-born English Test captain and all-rounder who settled in Australia at the time of World Series Cricket?

7. Which famous early Australian batsman and captain later migrated to England for whom he appeared in one Test match against South Africa?

8. Australia's first great strike bowler in Test cricket later migrated to England and became a director of a tea company. Who was he?

9. A post-war Australian left-arm wrist spinner had the unenviable Test bowling average of 165 after three

matches but later enjoyed an outstanding all-round career with Northamptonshire. Who was he?

10. One of Australia's greatest fast bowlers sandwiched his 10 Test career into a single calendar year at the age of thirty before moving to the Lancashire League and then to a highly successful county career with Lancashire. Who was he?

Frank Tyson

OF WHOM WAS IT SAID/WRITTEN?

1. 'He's so laid back he's comatose.'

2. 'He couldn't put a dent in a pound of butter.'

3. 'The corpse with pads on'

4. 'A cricketer of effect rather than the graces.'

5. 'The bowler of the century'

6. '[He] always seemed to think that the best possible change of attack was for him to give up bowling at one end and go on at the other.'

7. 'All his life he was facing the next ball.'

8. 'He was a batsman of high courage who used his physical advantages to the full.'

9. 'He was a marvellous blend of impish prankster, skilled batsman, clever tactician and sparkling speaker.'

10. 'Autocrat he may have been, but a benevolent autocrat nevertheless.'

11. 'He liked slapstick, but he knew when and to whom to throw the pie. His short, square build, busy movements and low geared run were made for comedy.'

12. 'No bowler ever cared less whether it rained or not.'

13. 'He batted perfectly because he was the perfect batsman.'

14. 'His forward defensive stroke was a complete statement.'

15. 'The ice-cold calculating brain of cricket.'

16. 'Crouch he certainly did, for style meant nothing to him.'

17. 'His batsmanship should have been weighted in carats not runs.'

18. 'He never bowled an ugly ball, and like all great bowlers he bowled precious few bad'uns either.'

19. 'He was born to rescue.'

20. 'As a saver of lost causes he has no rival.'

21. 'While he was there the game vibrated.'

22. 'He always played cricket as some proud Roman might have played it.'

23. 'A cavalier batsman and a roundhead captain.'

24. 'To hit him for four would arouse a belligerent ferocity which made you sorry.'

25. 'If he sniffed a crisis in the offing he made straight for it.'

26. 'He lived a corporate life in splendid isolation.'

27. 'He had no style and yet he is all style.'

28. 'He bowls like a god but he talks like a civil servant.'

29. 'His square cut was like the fall of a headsman's axe, clean and true.'

30. 'For years there was no bowler in the world against whom the best batsmen in the world would feel less secure, none who was more likely to produce a ball which left them helpless.'

Barmy Army celebrate England's
surprise victory at Adelaide, 1995.

FAMOUS GAMES

1. What were the two occasions when a side which was forced to follow on, won the match?

2. When England defeated Australia at Melbourne by 3 runs in the 1982-83 series who were the two Australian batsmen who added 70 runs for the last wicket to bring their side to the verge of victory?

3. Which lower-order English batsman cracked 88 runs to give his side a victory chance (which it took) on the final day of the Adelaide Test of 1994-95?

4. Which Australian all-rounder hit English off-spinner David Allen for 20 runs off an over to unsettle the English attack and open a victory opportunity for his side in the Old Trafford Test of 1961?

5. In what match did twenty wickets fall for 130 runs in an afternoon without a side being dismissed?

6. Australia drew the 1972 Test series in England two wins apiece after it gained a five-wicket victory at The Oval. Who were the two Australian batsmen whose undefeated partnership of 71 in the second innings brought their side that success?

7. Which match, involving the longest day in Test history (8 hours 3 minutes), saw England bowl out Australia in the final four hour session to win by 12 runs?

8. Who was the England hero in the final hour of the above game?

9. In a tightly fought game at The Oval in 1997 three bowlers achieved the remarkable performance of seven wickets in an innings. Who were they?

10. With the series tied 1-1 and Australia chasing 240 to win in its fourth innings at Melbourne in 1954-55 who broke the Australian innings apart to finish with the sensational figures of 7 for 27 on the final day?

Vic Richardson

WHO SAID THAT?
OR WAS REPUTED TO HAVE

1. 'Which bastard called this bastard a bastard'

2. 'There are two teams out there...'

3. '...naive and innocent'

4. 'This is war...'

5. 'The man's a pillock, a bloody great pillock'

6. '...that bugger Barnes'

7. 'Give me Arthur'

8. 'What do you think Arthur?'

9. 'I've got a little kid at home there who'll make it up for me.'

10. 'It's all happening...'

99's

1. Which Australian batsman made 99 in his Test debut at Trent Bridge?

2. Two English opening batsmen who frequently batted together are the only players to be run out for 99. Who are they?

3. Which English opening batsman is the only batsman to be not out on 99?

4. What is the only instance of two scores of 99 in a Test match?

5. Which three Australian middle-order batsmen have been dismissed for 99 at Lord's?

6. Who is the only English batsman to make 99 at Lord's

7. In which match was Keith Miller dismissed for 99?

8. In which match was Bob Cowper dismissed for 99?

9. Which English Test captain was dismissed for 99 at Brisbane in 1962-63?

10. Who is the only batsman to make 199 in an Ashes Test?

BOOKS, WRITERS, COMMENTATORS

1. Match the following:

It isn't Cricket	Phil Derriman
In the Fast Lane	Alan Davidson
The Demon Spofforth	Max Walker
Follow On	George Giffen
Fifteen Paces	Neville Cardus
Tangles	Richard Cashman
With Bat and Ball	Bruce Hamilton
Second Innings	Sid Barnes
Pro	Geoff Boycott
The Grand Old Ground	E.W. Swanton

2. Match the following:

The Willow Wand	Gideon Haigh
Cricket from the Grandstand	Edmund Blunden
Basingstoke Boy	Alan McGilvray
The Summer Game	Simon Raven
Cricket Country	Ray Robinson
The Game is Not the Same	John Arlott
Letting Rip	Keith Dunstan
Between Wickets	Derek Birley
Close of Play	Simon Wilde
The Paddock that Grew	Keith Miller

3. Match the following:

Willow Patterns	Brian Close
Turn of the Wheel	Alan Ross
Farewell to Cricket	Percy Fender
Batting from Memory	Bill Lawry
The Art of Captaincy	R.S. Whitington
Hutton and Washbrook	Don Bradman
Australia '55	A.A. Thomson

Time of the Tiger	Richie Benaud
I Don't Bruise Easily	Jack Fingleton
Run Digger	Mike Brearley

4. Which Australian commentator, journalist and author wrote biographies of Don Bradman, Richie Benaud and a history of Australian Cricket?

5. Which English commentators were known as 'Alderman' and 'Boil'?

6. Which member of the English radio commentary team is referred to as 'the Beard'?

7. When rain stopped play which English commentator was famous for talking about, as well as consuming, chocolate cake?

8. Which Australian Victory Test cricketer, later a journalist, co-wrote several books with former team-mate Keith Miller as well as producing biographies of Miller and Lindsay Hassett?

9. Which English Test player's wife wrote *Cricket XXXX Cricket* on the 1986-87 tour of Australia?

10. How many tour diaries has Steve Waugh published as books?
   (a) 6 (b) 8 (c) 10

Zzzzzz

1. Which English wicket-keeper took 95 minutes to open his score in the Adelaide Test of 1947?

2. Who was the English wicket-keeper whose innings of 3 took 100 minutes at the Sydney Test of 1962-63?

3. Which English opening batsman had scored 66 half an hour after tea on the opening day of the Perth Test of 1982 and remained undefeated on that score ninety minutes later at stumps.

4. What is the fewest runs scored in a full day's play?

5. Which Australian opening batsman batted 250 minutes while scoring 28 runs at Brisbane in 1958-59?

6. Who faced 337 balls in 449 minutes while scoring 77 runs and struck just one boundary at Perth in 1978?

7. What are the only occasions when no wickets fell in a full day's play?

8. How many balls did Australian opener Alick Bannerman face in his marathon innings of 91 at Sydney in 1891-92?
(a) 420 (b) 520 (c) 620

9. Alick Bannerman's career scoring rate of between 22 and 23 runs per hundred balls was matched by which Englishman?
(a) Billy Scotton (b) Trevor Bailey (c) Mike Brearley

10. Three Test matches have been abandoned without a ball being bowled. Where and when were they due to have been played?

The Answers

Ashes

1. King Cole
2. The Oval
3. William Murdoch (Australia) and A.N. Hornby (England)
4. Frederick Spofforth
5. *Sporting Times*
6. Hon. Ivo Bligh
7. Florence Morphy
8. Clarence Percival Moody
9. Pelham Warner
10. Bicentennial Test match held in Sydney in 1988.

First Test

1. Alfred Shaw
2. 0
3. Harry Jupp who scored 63 in the first innings.
4. George Ulyett
5. The 6 Victorians and 5 New South Welshmen practised independently.
6. Melbourne
7. Felix
8. 49 years 119 days
9. E.J. 'Ned' Gregory
10. Allen Hill

Captains

1. James Lillywhite
2. Colin Cowdrey
3. Fairy Meadow
4. Mike Brearley
5. Lord Harris
6. Peter May, 1961. The professional/amateur distinction in English cricket ended in 1962.
7. James Lillywhite, Alfred Shaw, Arthur Shrewsbury. W.G.Grace is a reasonable wrong answer.
8. Tom Horan, Percy McDonnell

9. Arthur Jones (1907-08), Pelham Warner (1911-12)
10. 1905, 1909
11. Stanley Jackson, Monty Noble, Lindsay Hassett
12. Mike Denness
13. Ted Dexter
14. Barry Jarman
15. Herbie Collins. Australia lost the Fifth Test at The Oval in 1926 and the rain-ruined series 0-1.
16. Jack Ryder
17. Percy Chapman, Brisbane 1928-29
18. Percy McDonnell, Sydney 1886-87. Australia lost by 13 runs.
19. Hon. Ivo Bligh, 23 years 292 days, 1882-83
20. William Murdoch, 24 years 324 days, 1880
21. Michael Atherton
22. Graham Yallop, Mike Brearley
23. England won 5-1
24. Len Hutton
25. Baddeley, John Knight, Maldon, Colin
26. 188 by Mike Denness, Sixth Test, Melbourne 1975
27. 240 by Wally Hammond, Lord's 1938
28. 270 by Don Bradman, Melbourne 1937
29. 311 by Bob Simpson, Old Trafford 1964
30. William Murdoch (1880, 1882, 1884, 1890)
31. Joe Darling (1899, 1902, 1905); Allan Border (1985, 1989, 1993); Arthur Shrewsbury (1884-85, 1886-87, 1887-88).
32. 1, Dave Gregory in the first Test of 1877
33. 11
34. Bill Lawry made 60 not out of his team's 116 in the second innings of the Third Test at Sydney in 1970-71 and he was omitted following the Fifth Test of the series.
35. John Edrich
36. Brian Booth
37. Mike Gatting 1986-87
38. Adam Gilchrist

39. Norman Yardley
40. Warwick Armstrong 1920-21

Batting

1. W.G. Grace
2. Reg Foster, 287
3. Greg Blewett
4. Gilbert Jessop
5. Bill Ponsford
6. Clem Hill
7. 1901-02
8. Joe Darling, Adelaide 1898
9. Les Favell
10. Graham Gooch 133, Old Trafford 1993
11. G.F. (Fred) Grace, The Oval 1880
12. Percy McDonnell, Sydney 1882-83
13. Wally Hammond 905, 1928-29; Don Bradman (twice) 974, 1930 and 810, 1936-37; Mark Taylor 839, 1989. Taylor achieved his total in a six Test series.
14. Herbert Sutcliffe 1924-25, Wally Hammond 1928-29, Don Bradman 1930.
15. Joe Darling 1897-98
16. Don Bradman (thrice) 1930, 1936-37, 1938; Arthur Morris (twice) 1946-47, 1948; Michael Slater (twice) 1994-95, 1998-99
17. Jack Hobbs 1911-12
18. Jack Hobbs (twice) 1911-12, 1924-25
19. David Gower 1985, Chris Broad 1986-87, Michael Vaughan 2002-03
20. Joe Darling 1897-98
21. Clem Hill 1901-02
22. Don Bradman
23. Warren Bardsley, The Oval 1909; Arthur Morris, Adelaide 1946-47; Steve Waugh, Old Trafford 1997; Matthew Hayden, Brisbane 2002-03.

24. Herbert Sutcliffe, Melbourne 1924-25; Wally Hammond, Adelaide, 1928-29; Denis Compton, Adelaide 1946-47
25. J.E. Barrett 67*, Lord's 1890; Bobby Abel 132*, Sydney 1891-92
26. Bill Lawry, 60*, Sydney, 1970-71; Geoff Boycott 99*, Perth 1979-80
27. Bill Woodfull 30*, Brisbane, 1928-29; 73*, Adelaide, 1932-33
28. Denis Compton, 562, 1948
29. Herbert Sutcliffe 66.85; Ken Barrington 63.96
30. They each scored a ninety in their first Test.
31. They each made their initial first-class century in a Test match.
32. Graham Yallop
33. Bob Simpson and Bill Lawry
34. Kim Hughes
35. Rev. David Sheppard
36. Graham Thorpe, Trent Bridge 1993
37. Nasser Hussain 207, Edgbaston 1997
38. Justin Langer 250, Melbourne, 2002-03
39. David Gower, 732 runs, 1985 (six Tests)
40. Michael Vaughan 633 runs, 2002-03
41. Victor Trumper, Old Trafford, 1902; Charlie Macartney, Headingley, 1926; Don Bradman, Headingley, 1930
42. Kumar Shri Ranjitsinhji, Old Trafford, 1896; Phil Mead, The Oval, 1921
43. England, Trent Bridge 1938
44. Australia, Lord's 1993
45. Jack Hobbs, 142, Melbourne 1928-29
46. Matthew Hayden, Damien Martyn
47. Dean Jones
48. 475
49. Australia, Fifth Test, The Oval, 1st day 1934
50. Fourth Test, Old Trafford 1964

Bowling

1. John Snow
2. Ernie Jones
3. Warwick Armstrong
4. Bernard Bosanquet
5. Leslie O'Brien Fleetwood-Smith took 1 for 298, The Oval 1938
6. Ian Peebles 6 for 204, The Oval 1930
7. Herbert Hordern
8. Bruce Reid
9. Tony Lock, Jim Burke
10. Clarrie Grimmett
11. Alan Connolly
12. Frederick Spofforth, 13 for 110, Melbourne 1878-79
13. Two Australian bowlers in the same innings at The Oval, 1880. George Palmer 1 for 116 and Alick Bannerman 3 for 111.
14. Albert 'Tibby' Cotter 0 for 125, Melbourne 1911-12
15. Shane Warne 11 for 229, The Oval, 2001
16. Andrew Caddick 10 for 215, Sydney 2002-03
17. Clarrie Grimmett 11-82, Sydney 1924-25; Bob Massie 16-137, Lord's 1972
18. Albert Trott 8-43, Adelaide 1894-95
19. Frederick Martin 12 for 102, The Oval 1890; Ken Farnes 10 for 179, Trent Bridge 1934
20. Shane Warne, Melbourne, 1994-95; Darren Gough, Sydney, 1998-99.
21. Arthur Mailey 36, 1920-21. Mailey bowled in only four matches.
22. Bobby Peel 102 at 16.98; Charles Turner 101 at 16.53
23. Hugh Trumble, Melbourne 1901-02 and 1903-04
24. Fred Spofforth, Melbourne 1878-79
25. Lindsay Kline
26. Wilfred Rhodes (31, 1903-04) and Frank Foster (32, 1911-12) for England, and Jack Saunders for Australia (31, 1907-08)

27. Sydney Barnes 5.3
28. Charlie Turner 5.9
29. Jack White delivered 749 balls to take 13 wickets for 256 runs in the 1929 Test match at Adelaide Oval.
30. Tom Veivers sent down 571 balls to take 3 wickets for 155 in the only English innings at Old Trafford in 1964.
31. Tom Richardson
32. Fred Spofforth, Dennis Lillee
33. Dennis Lillee 167; Ian Botham 148.
34. Jim Laker 46, 1956; Terry Alderman 42, 1981. Alderman played six Tests.
35. Terry Alderman 1981, 1989. Each series comprised six Tests.
36. Rodney Hogg 41, 1978-79; Maurice Tate 38, 1924-25. Hogg played six Tests.
37. Arthur Mailey did so twice. He took 10-302 at Adelaide in 1920-21 and 7-308 at Sydney in 1924-25.
38. England, The Oval 1884. Australia made 551.
39. Arthur Mailey and Clarrie Grimmett
40. Frank Allan

All-Rounders

1. Jack Gregory 100 and 7-69, Melbourne 1920-21; Ian Botham 149 not out and 6-95, Leeds 1981
2. Charles Kelleway
3. Wilfred Rhodes
4. George Giffen 1894-95
5. George Giffen, First Test, Sydney 1894-95
6. Ian Botham 399 runs, 34 wickets, 1981; 250 runs, 31 wickets, 1985
7. George Giffen, Monty Noble
8. Wilfred Rhodes, Ian Botham
9. Charlie Macartney
10. Richie Benaud, Alan Davidson

Wicket-keepers

1. Jack Blackham, Barry Jarman and Adam Gilchrist (Australia); Alec Stewart (England)
2. Alfred Lyttleton, The Oval 1884
3. Hampton 'Hammy' Love
4. Arthur McIntyre
5. Hanson Carter
6. George Duckworth
7. Bert Oldfield, Arthur Lilley
8. Ben Barnett
9. Rod Marsh, Centenary Test 1977
10. Ian Healy, Adam Gilchrist
11. Les Ames, Allan Knott, Jack Richards, Jack Russell
12. E.J. Kenneth Burn
13. Gil Langley
14. Charlie Walker
15. Tim Zoehrer
16. Rod Marsh 1982-83 in a six Test series
17. Bob Taylor 1970-71, 1974-75, 1978-79, 1979-80, 1982-83
18. David Bairstow
19. Wayne Phillips
20. Les Ames, 102 centuries

Twelfth Men

1. John Edwards
2. First Test, Melbourne 1881-82
3. Leslie Poidevin
4. Don Bradman
5. Ken Meuleman
6. Ian McLachlan
7. Bob Cowper, 307 at Melbourne in 1965-66
8. Terry Jenner
9. He had taken 7 wickets for 111 in the previous Test in Perth including figures of 5 for 88 in the second innings.
10. Ray Bright, Graham Barlow

Centenary Test (Melbourne)

1. Greg Chappell, Tony Greig
2. 167
3. Lead. England was dismissed for 95.
4. David Hookes
5. Tom Brooks, Max O'Connell
6. Derek Randall, who made a brilliant 174 in the second innings.
7. Rick McCosker
8. Dennis Lillee
9. 45 runs
10. 218

Scandals

1. Victor Trumper, Clem Hill, Warwick Armstrong, Hanson Carter, Albert 'Tibby' Cotter, Vernon Ransford
2. Frank Laver
3. David Gower and John Morris
4. Roy Park
5. Clem Hill
6. Arthur Coningham
7. Freddie Brown
8. Lord Mayor of Brisbane
9. George Davis
10. 500/1
11. Syphilis
12. Ernest Jones
13. Merv Hughes
14. Aluminium Bat Incident
15. Ray Illingworth
16. Geoff Boycott
17. He had his hands in his pockets
18. Harry Donnan
19. Sid Barnes
20. Terry Alderman
21. Frank Ward

22. Edward Pooley
23. Percy McDonnell and Billy Barnes
24. Graeme Hick
25. Bert Ironmonger
26. Tony Lock
27. Ian Meckiff
28. Jack House
29. Walter Giffen
30. Clem Hill and Peter McAlister

Families

1. The Grace brothers initials are E.M., W.G. and G.F.
2. The Chappell brothers initials are I.M., G.S. and T.M.
3. William Gunn and George Gunn; Joe Hardstaff snr and Joe Hardstaff jnr
4. Ian Johnson
5. Craig White and Darren Lehmann
6. Bob Simpson
7. Steve Waugh
8. Terry and Denise Alderman
9. William Cooper
10. Adam and Ben Hollioake, Trent Bridge 1997

Umpires

1. James Phillips, Bob Crockett
2. Max O'Connell
3. Frank Chester
4. George Coulthard, Paddy McShane
5. Charles Bannerman
6. Mel McInnes
7. Lou Rowan
8. Peter Willey
9. Ernest Jones
10. Jim Phillips, Second Test, Melbourne 1897-98

General

1. Johnny Douglas
2. Mike Smith (rugby union)
3. Martin McCague
4. Bruce Francis
5. Peter May's 1958-59 touring team
6. Once (1934)
7. Sammy Woods
8. Keith Stackpole
9. Tom Groube, Clarrie Grimmett, Brendon Julian
10. Brisbane Cricket Ground (Woollongabba), 1950-51 series
11. Dobbin
12. C.L. 'Jack' Badcock
13. 1964
14. Jack Crawford
15. Denis Compton
16. Ray Robinson
17. Members of Parliament
18. 211, 254. These are the progressive highest individual innings by Australian batsmen in Test matches.
19. 170, 287. These are the progressive highest individual innings by English batsmen in Test matches.
20. Archie Jackson
21. Durtanovich
22. Stephen Harold Gascoigne
23. Leslie Fleetwood-Smith
24. 1928-29, 1932-33
25. First Test and Fourth Tests, Melbourne Cricket Ground, 1881-82. Although both games were called 'timeless' the English players' departure for New Zealand prevented the first match being finished, and rain on the final day plus tight scheduling of a country match caused the second to be called off.
26. Doug Wright
27. The 'Second Bradman'
28. Sir Pelham Warner, Sir Jack Hobbs, Sir Leonard Hutton, Sir Colin Cowdrey (later Lord Cowdrey)

29. Bob Willis
30. 1920-21
31. 1899
32. 1903-04, 1974-75
33. Wilfred Rhodes 1899-1926
34. Syd Gregory 1890-1912
35. 1936-37
36. Michael Atherton
37. Steve Waugh
38. Adelaide
39. The first Limited Over International match
40. Richard Stilgoe
41. Earl Sheffield 1891-92, Duke of Norfolk 1962-63
42. 1978-79
43. Syd Copley. Copley played his only first-class game (for Nottinghamshire) that season.
44. 1884-85, England
45. 28, 1884-85
46. 30, 1921
47. Arthur and Victor Richardson
48. Brian Booth
49. Herbert Vere 'Bert' Evatt
50. Sid Barnes

Good Beginnings, Bad Starts, Bad Endings

1. Reg Foster 306 (287, 19), Sydney 1903-04
2. Kepler Wessels 208 (162, 46), Brisbane 1982-83; Archie Jackson 200 (164, 36) Adelaide, 1928-29
3. Jim Burke
4. Harry Graham
5. Reg Duff
6. Bright's Disease
7. Albert Trott
8. Albert Cotter
9. Dennis Amiss, Graham Gooch
10. Denis Compton

Don Bradman

1. 28, 187
2. 5
3. 2nd wicket with Bill Ponsford, 451; 3rd wicket with Lindsay Hassett, 276; 4th wicket with Bill Ponsford, 388; 5th wicket with Sid Barnes, 405; 6th wicket with Jack Fingleton, 346.
4. Brisbane Exhibition Ground, 1928
5. 18 and 1
6. Maurice Tate
7. He became the youngest player (at 20 years 129 days) to score a Test century for Australia. It was a record he held only briefly as Archie Jackson broke it in the following Test.
8. 254, Lord's 1930
9. Wally Hammond
10. Walter Robins
11. Bill Bowes, Gubby Allen, Bill Voce, Alec Bedser, Eric Hollies
12. Alec Bedser's delivery which bowled him for a duck in the Adelaide Test of 1947.
13. Alec Bedser, Len Hutton
14. 'Fancy doing that'
15. Sid Barnes
16. Hedley Verity
17. Jack O'Hagan
18. 89.78
19. 10. Brisbane Exhibition Ground, Brisbane Cricket Ground (Woollongabba), Sydney Cricket Ground, Melbourne Cricket Ground, Adelaide Oval, Trent Bridge, Lord's, Headingley, Old Trafford, The Oval.
20. Their longest Test innings each lasted 458 minutes. Bradman scored 270 at Melbourne in 1936-37 and Bailey 68 at Brisbane in 1958-59.

Bodyline

1. Hugh Buggy
2. Winchester/Oxford
3. Frank Foster
4. Melbourne High School
5. Bob Wyatt, Nawab of Pataudi, Gubby Allen, Freddie Brown
6. Nawab of Pataudi
7. Harold Larwood, Bill Voce, Gubby Allen, Bill Bowes, Maurice Tate
8. The amateur Gubby Allen refused to bowl it. The professional Maurice Tate is reputed to have refused to bowl it and was not called upon during the series. Bill Bowes played only one Test (Melbourne) and took one wicket (Bradman) for the series.
9. Stan McCabe's
10. Twelfth man
11. Pelham Warner, Richard Palairet
12. Eddie Gilbert
13. 56
14. 33 wickets at 19
15. Stanley Bruce
16. Rockley Wilson. Wilson was a master at Winchester and ran the cricket program when Jardine attended the school. He was also an all-rounder who played one Test for England at Sydney in 1920-21.
17. Gary Sweet, Hugo Weaving, Jim Holt
18. Bill Ferguson
19. Tim Wall
20. George Hele, George Borwick

Grounds

1. The Oval, 1880.
2. Don Bradman, M.A. Monty Noble, Bill O'Reilly, Doug Walters
3. Bramall Lane, Sheffield; Exhibition Ground, Brisbane

4. Headingley, Brisbane Cricket Ground (Woollongabba), Melbourne Cricket Ground, The Oval (Kennington)
5. Adelaide Oval, Old Trafford
6. Lord's
7. Cathedral End
8. Old Trafford (Bert Flack); SCG (Athol Watkins); Lord's (Mick Hunt); Adelaide Oval (Les Burdett)
9. The Oval 1938
10. Lord's 1930
11. Sydney 1886-87
12. Edgbaston 1902
13. Adelaide Oval 1920-21
14. Melbourne 1928-29
15. Innings and 579 runs
16. Innings and 332 runs
17. Brisbane Exhibition Ground
18. The Oval
19. Lord's
20. An afternoon breeze in Perth
21. Adelaide Oval 1884-85
22. Lord's 1888
23. Old Trafford 1888. England won before lunch on the second day by an innings and 21 runs.
24. Headingley 1948
25. The Oval 1902, Melbourne 1907-08
26. Old Trafford 1902, Melbourne 1982-83
27. Sydney Cricket Ground
28. Melbourne Cricket Ground
29. WACA Ground, Perth
30. Old Trafford

Invincibles

1. 721
2. They dismissed Australia in a single day.
3. Arthur Morris
4. Ray Lindwall and Bill Johnston tied with 27 each.

5. Sid Barnes
6. George Emmett. Aged 36, he made 10 and 0 in his only Test although he continued to play county cricket for Gloucestershire for a further eleven years.
7. Ron Saggers
8. Jim Laker
9. Lindwall took 6 for 20 as he blitzed England for 52 in their first innings. Arthur Morris made 196 in Australia's only innings.
10. Colin McCool, Ron Hamence

One Test Wonders

1. Ray Robinson
2. Keith Slater
3. Shaun Young
4. Peter Allan
5. Paul Parker and James Whittaker
6. Arnie Sidebottom
7. Mick Malone
8. Fred Freer
9. Arnold Warren
10. Mervyn Harvey

Young and Old

1. Tom Garrett, 18 years 232 days, Melbourne 1876-77
2. 13
3. W.G. Grace, 50 years 320 days, Trent Bridge 1899
4. Bert Ironmonger, 49 years 327 days, Sydney 1932-33
5. Jack Hobbs, 6
6. Archie Jackson, Neil Harvey, Doug Walters
7. Jack Ferris 5-76, Sydney 1886-87; Craig McDermott (twice) 1985
8. 1. Ben Hollioake, 19 years and 269 days, Trent Bridge 1997
9. Arthur Richardson 100, Headingley 1926
10. Hanson Carter

On Tour

1. Victor Trumper 2570, 1902
2. Fred Spofforth
3. Charles Turner 283, 1888. Fred Spofforth 201, 1884. Jack Ferris took 199 wickets on the 1888 tour.
4. Bill Johnston 102, 1948
5. Bill Lawry 2019, 1961
6. Don Bradman 115.66, 1938; Bill Johnston 102, 1953; Damien Martyn 104.66, 2001
7. Jim Higgs, 1975. Higgs played eight matches but had only two innings, one of which was not out.
8. Victor Trumper, Charlie Macartney, Don Bradman, Bob Simpson
9. Frank Woolley, Colin Cowdrey
10. Don Bradman 2960, 1930; Victor Trumper 2570, 1902
11. Don Bradman 1930, 1934, 1938, 1948; Warren Bardsley 1909, 1912, 1921
12. Ernie McCormick
13. George Lohmann, 1886-87
14. Two separate touring parties known as G.F. Vernon's Team and Lillywhite, Shaw and Shrewsbury's Team combined to play as a single side.
15. Kumar Shri Ranjitsinhji, 1897-98
16. Maurice Tate 77, 1924-25
17. Patsy Hendren 1920-21, 1924-25, 1928-29
18. Frank Tyson 51, 1954-55
19. Wally Hammond 1553, 1928-29; Geoff Boycott 1535, 1970-71
20. Geoff Boycott, 1970-71

Odd Selections/Non-Selections

1. Peter Taylor
2. Sydney Callaway
3. Johnny Wardle
4. Albert Trott
5. Mike Whitney

6. Ken Eastwood
7. Ernie Bromley
8. Charlie Parker
9. Fred Trueman
10. Colin Cowdrey

Nick and Other Names

1. Charles (Terror) Turner; A.N. (Monkey) Hornby; Hunter (Stork) Hendry; Pelham (Plum) Warner; Leslie (Chuck) Fleetwood-Smith; Geoff (Noddy) Pullar; Wally (Griz) Grout; Derek (Arkle) Randall; Wayne (Flipper) Phillips; David (Biggles) Gower.
2. Ted (Lord Ted) Dexter, Keith (Nugget) Miller, A.P. (Tich) Freeman, Bill (Phantom) Lawry, Fred and Maurice (Chub) Tate, Neil (Ninna) Harvey, Geoff (Dusty) Miller, Henry (Tup) Scott, Reggie (Tip) Foster, Graham (Sledge) Corling.
3. Johnny Won't Hit Today, Please Go Home
4. Derek (Deadly) Underwood, Monty (Mary Ann) Noble, Edward (Nobby) Clarke, Alan (Claw) Davidson, Colin (Ollie) Milburn, Bill (Tiger) O'Reilly and E.J. (Tiger) Smith, Harold (Lol) Larwood, Rod (Iron Gloves) Marsh, Gary (Gus) Gilmour and Angus (Gus) Fraser.
5. Keith (Gnome) Fletcher and Clarrie (Gnome) Grimmett, Max (Tangles) Walker, Jack (Farmer) White, Kerry (Skull) O'Keefe, Geoff (Horse) Arnold, Albert (Tibby) Cotter, Brian (George) Statham, Ken (Slasher) Mackay, Frank (Typhoon) Tyson, Jason (Dizzy) Gillespie.
6. Trevor (Barnacle) Bailey, Jack (Big Jake) Iverson, Ian (Beefy) Botham, Herbert (Horseshoe) Collins, Kumar Shri Ranjitsinhji (Smith), Bert (Dainty) Ironmonger, Elias (Patsy) Hendren, Darren (Boof) Lehmann, David (Mumbles) Lloyd, Steve (Tugga) Waugh.
7. Percy (Greatheart) McDonnell, Mark (Junior) Waugh, Ashley (Rowdy) Mallett, Arthur (Affie) Jarvis, Ricky (Punter) Ponting, Graham (Garth) McKenzie, Terry

(Clem) Alderman, Lindsay (Spinner) Kline, Greg (Mo) Matthews, Johnny (Cho) Gleeson.

8. W.G. (The Champion) Grace, E.M. (The Coroner) Grace, Gilbert (The Croucher) Jessop, Jack (The Master) Hobbs, Douglas (The Iron Duke) Jardine, Fred (The Demon) Spofforth, George (The Australian Hercules) Bonnor, Warwick (The Big Ship) Armstrong, Vic (The Guardsman) Richardson and Don (The Don) Bradman.

9. Clayvel Lindsay 'Jack' Badcock, Edwin James Kenneth Burn, Warwick Maxwell 'Rick' Darling, John Ross Frederick Duncan, Donald Raeburn Algernon Gehrs, Arthur Theodore Wallace Grout, Michael Joseph 'Roger' Hartigan, Robert Neil Harvey, Arthur Lindsay Hassett, Robert John Inverarity, William Albert Stanley Oldfield, Andrew Paul Sheahan, George Henry Stevens Trott, John William Trumble, Thomas Welbourn 'Tim' Wall, Kevin Douglas Walters.

10. John Michael Brearley, Arthur Percy Frank Chapman, Michael Colin Cowdrey, Horace Edgar 'Tom' Dollery, Thomas Godfrey Evans, George Frederick Grace, Elias Henry 'Patsy' Hendren, William Eric Hollies, Francis Stanley Jackson, Graham Anthony Richard Lock, Charles Philip Mead, Robert Walter Vivian Robins, John Brian Statham.

Who am I?

1. Jack Fingleton
2. Tony Dell
3. Bob Willis
4. Rick Darling
5. Reg Allen
6. Neil Hawke and Eric Freeman
7. Geoff Lawson
8. Ron Hamence
9. Douglas Carr
10. William Midwinter

Emigrants

1. Peter Sleep
2. Tony Lock
3. Frank Tyson
4. Harold Larwood
5. Bill Alley
6. Tony Greig
7. Billy Murdoch
8. Fred Spofforth
9. George Tribe
10. Ted McDonald

Of Whom was it Said/Written?

1. David Gower by Penny Edmonds
2. Harold Larwood by Ernie Jones
3. Bill Lawry by Denis Compton
4. Ian Chappell by John Arlott
5. Frank Allan
6. George Giffen by W.G. Grace
7. W.G. Grace by A.A. Thomson
8. Tony Greig by E.W. Swanton
9. Lindsay Hassett by Jack Pollard.
10. Lord Hawke by John Marshall
11. Patsy Hendren by R.C. Robertson-Glasgow
12. George Hirst by E.H.D. Sewell
13. Jack Hobbs by John Arlott
14. Len Hutton by Harold Pinter
15. Ray Illingworth by John Hampshire
16. Gilbert Jessop by Johnny Moyes
17. Alan Kippax by Ray Robinson
18. Jim Laker by Robin Marlar
19. Maurice Leyland by R.C. Robertson-Glasgow
20. Stan McCabe by Ray Robinson
21. Charlie Macartney by Johnny Moyes
22. Archie MacLaren by Neville Cardus
23. Peter May by A.A. Thomson

24. Bill O'Reilly by Sir Donald Bradman
25. Eddie Paynter by Ronald Mason
26. Herbert Sutcliffe by J.M. Kilburn
27. Victor Trumper by G.W. Beldam and C.B. Fry
28. Derek Underwood by Michael Davie
29. Cyril Washbrook by Margaret Hughes
30. Douglas Wright by R.L. Arrowsmith

Famous Games

1. Sydney 1894, Leeds 1981
2. Allan Border and Jeff Thomson
3. Philip de Freitas
4. Alan Davidson
5. Brisbane, 1950-51. Batting on a 'sticky' wicket England captain Freddie Brown declared his side's first innings closed at 7-68, Australian captain Lindsay Hassett closed his second innings at 7-32, and England was 6-30 in its second innings at stumps.
6. Paul Sheahan and Rod Marsh
7. Fourth Test, Melbourne 1998-99
8. Dean Headley who took 4-4 in his second spell and 6-60 for the innings.
9. Glenn McGrath, Philip Tufnell, Michael Kasprowicz
10. Frank Tyson

Who Said That?
(or was reputed to have)

1. Vic Richardson to Douglas Jardine
2. Bill Woodfull to Pelham Warner and Richard Palairet
3. Shane Warne and Mark Waugh to Adelaide Oval press conference, 1998-99.
4. Wally Hammond to Don Bradman
5. Fred Trueman on Ian Botham (while broadcasting) when Botham was caught off Bob Holland in the Lord's Test in 1985 after having made 85.
6. Archie MacLaren on Sydney Barnes

7. WG Grace asking first for Arthur Shrewsbury when picking a Test side.
8. Vic Richardson in commentary pairing with Arthur Gilligan
9. Fred Tate
10. Bill Lawry's signature phrase while broadcasting.

99s

1. Arthur Chipperfield, 1934
2. Graham Gooch, Melbourne 1979-80; Michael Atherton, Lord's 1993
3. Geoff Boycott, Perth 1979-80
4. Kim Hughes and Geoff Boycott, Perth 1979-80
5. Charlie Macartney, 1912; Ross Edwards, 1975; Mark Waugh, 1993.
6. Eddie Paynter, 1938
7. Fourth Test, Adelaide 1950-51
8. Second Test, Melbourne 1965-66
9. Ted Dexter
10. Matthew Elliott, Headingley 1997

Books and Writers

1. Sid Barnes, *It isn't Cricket*; Geoff Boycott, *In the Fast Lane*; Richard Cashman, *The Demon Spofforth*; E.W. Swanton, *Follow On*; Alan Davidson, *Fifteen Paces*; Max Walker, *Tangles*; George Giffen, *With Bat and Ball*; Neville Cardus, *Second Innings*; Bruce Hamilton, *Pro*; Phil Derriman, *The Grand Old Ground*.
2. Derek Birley, *The Willow Wand*; Keith Miller, *Cricket from the Grandstand*; John Arlott, *Basingstoke Boy*; Gideon Haigh, *The Summer Game*; Edmund Blunden, *Cricket Country*; Alan McGilvray, *The Game is Not the Same;* Simon Wilde, *Letting Rip*; Ray Robinson, *Between Wickets*; Simon Raven, *Close of Play*; Keith Dunstan, *The Paddock that Grew*.

3. Richie Benaud, *Willow Patterns*; Percy Fender, *Turn of the Wheel*; Don Bradman, *Farewell to Cricket*; Jack Fingleton, *Batting from Memory*; Mike Brearley, *The Art of Captaincy*; A.A. Thomson, *Hutton and Washbrook*; Alan Ross, *Australia '55*; R.S. Whitington, *Time of the Tiger*; Brian Close, *I Don't Bruise Easily*; Bill Lawry, *Run Digger*.
4. A.G. 'Johnny' Moyes
5. Don Mosey, Trevor Bailey
6. Bill Frindall
7. Brian Johnston
8. R.S. Whitington
9. Phil Edmonds
10. 10

Zzzzzzz

1. Godfrey Evans
2. John Murray
3. Chris Tavare
4. England 8-106, Brisbane 1958-59
5. Jim Burke
6. Geoff Boycott
7. England 0-283, Melbourne 1924-25; Australia, 0-301, Trent Bridge 1989
8. 620
9. Billy Scotton
10. Old Trafford (twice) 1890, 1938; Melbourne 1970-71

Brief Bibliography

Peter Arnold and Peter Wynne-Thomas, *An Ashes Anthology – England v Australia*, London, 1989

Ralph Barker and Irving Rosenwater, *Test Cricket, England v Australia*, London, 1969

Charles Davis, *Test Cricket in Australia: The Test Match Archive*, Melbourne, 2002

Ross Dundas with Jack Pollard, *Australian Cricket: Highest, Most and Best*, Sydney, 1995

Richard Cashman et al. (eds), *The Oxford Companion to Australian Cricket*, Melbourne, 1995

Roderick Easdale, *England's One Test Wonders*, 1999

Bill Frindall, *The Wisden Book of Cricket Records*, London, 1981

David Frith, *England Versus Australia Test Match Records 1877-1985*, London, 1986

David Lemmon, *The Wisden Book of Cricket Quotations*, London, 1982

Christopher Martin-Jenkins, *The Complete Who's Who of Test Cricketers*, London, 1980

Jack Pollard, *Australian Cricket: The Game and the Players*, Sydney, 1982

Ray Webster, *Australian First-Class Cricket Vols. I and II*, Melbourne, 1991, 1997

Peter Wynne-Thomas, *The Complete History of Cricketers on Tour: At Home and Abroad*, London, 1989

Allan's Cricket Annual
Wisden Cricketers' Almanack
Wisden Cricketers' Almanack Australia
www.cricinfo.com